Musings of a Patriot

A Collection of Essays on Liberia

Momoh Sekou Dudu

M & M Publishers

Dedication

This work is dedicated to the people of the republic of Liberia.

Any error(s) of commission and/or omission in this work are entirely the author's.

Table of Contents

ACKNOWLEDGEMENTS

I am eternally grateful to all my teachers who, all through my educational experience, have awakened in me a sense of curiosity not to be content with first answers but to consistently and persistently inquire a little further.

And to my many students over the years, I can't thank you all enough for challenging me, always, to engage more, and to think just a bit deeper each time.

Author's Note

I am a stickler for documentation. This is a trait, I'd like to think, I've developed over more than a decade in the school setting both as an instructor and as an administrator. In that arena, "what is not documented is not done" is much more than a phrase in passing; careers are made or lost on account of it.

And, there is nothing more worthy of documentation, in my mind, than views — written and spoken — about the entity to which I owe my greatest allegiance: The Republic of Liberia. When it comes to Liberia, I hold myself as responsible and accountable as I hold others. I want to be able to look back, after the fact, and take stock of positions I'd represented in the past, to claim vindication, and to acknowledge my wrongs, where necessary.

Musings of a Patriot is a result of this conscious effort on my part. A short anthology of my thoughts on governance in Liberia, it brings together under one cover the occasional insights I have shared via various Liberian Online Magazines and listservs over the last decade. Some of these writings were precipitated by happenings in the corridors of power in Liberia while others were purely results of deep thoughts and reflections as I pondered the future of my country.

I hope this short work offers you your very own contemplative moment and spur you on to a more active participatory role in the national debate for a secured future for Liberia and Liberians.

Momoh Sekou Dudu

Otsego, Minnesota

United States of America

September 10, 2014

Essays

In Taylor's Liberia, a Culture of Impunity Thrives

On July 19, 1997 war-wearied Liberians flocked to the polls to elect a core of post-war political leaders. Overwhelmingly, they elected Charles Taylor, the architect of the brutal civil war, as president of the plundered nation. Political pundits the world over found it difficult to fathom this outcome. After all, was it not this same Taylor who had rained terror on every facet of the country as if there would be no tomorrow? Were Liberians so traumatized that they'd reward the messenger of evil with the presidency? Wasn't July 19 their chance to reject the policy of banditry?

To the minds fortunate not to have been subdued by the cruelty of the Liberian carnage, yes, the majority of Liberians were fools not to have sent the war-baron packing. But, for those of us that were in Monrovia then, we heard many Liberians offer a somber rationale for voting the National Patriotic Party (NPP) and its leader, Charles McArthur Taylor to power. The reason, taken in its totality, established the following premise:

First, Taylor's penchant for power, no matter whether it took wiping out most Liberians to acquire it, was insatiable. Second, if Taylor was balloted out of the presidency, it was more than certain that he would resuscitate the war. Third, the NPP had pilfered so much of the nation's resources, it only made sense to get it elected so that the amassed wealth would be expended on the reconstruction of the country.

This line of thought might sound very counterintuitive. Nevertheless, it appealed to the majority of the post-war electorate; and, it eventually propelled Taylor and his unruly army of ex-NPFL rebels to resounding victory — 'free and fair' victory, in the language of the international observers who monitored the elections. Only a higher power can judge these "experts." I cannot but wonder why there is a tribunal in The Hague prosecuting war criminals instead of letting them run for elective offices, as was abetted in Liberia?

So, out of fear of taking the country back to war, Liberians elected a war monger, hoping against all hope, that he would reconstruct the bleeding nation with his spoils of war. Ever since his election in 1997, Taylor has shown no such inclination. To the contrary, he has declared war on civility in our country; he has continued to torture, disappear, and kill-off his perceived enemies. His elaborate criminal gang, composed of a violent security apparatus and murderous band of operatives, are practically commissioned to silence the people, whatever that might require. If it means death for the targeted citizen(s), so be it. After all, anything goes in Taylor's Liberia. Indeed, a violent culture of impunity has been unleashed on the country. If for one second it crosses your mind that this is too broad a charge, just consider the following incidents:

(1). With the tacit approval of Charles Taylor, members of his dreaded special Security Service (SSS), in 1997, kidnapped former ally turned opposition politician Samuel Saye Dokie, his wife and two other family members. These poor souls were brutally tortured and eventually burnt to death. Since this gruesome murder, the government has done nothing to bring the culprits to book.

(2). In 1998, Nowah Flomo, a poor market woman, toiling to make ends meet, was forced out of her home by government security forces. She has never been seen since and is presumed dead. Again, the perpetrators of this heinous act are going about their lives in Monrovia as if nothing happened.

(3). Journalists Alex Reed and Hassan Bility of the defunct National Newspaper were also brutally manhandled in 1997 and 1998 respectively. Their crimes: Reed dared to inquire about the murder of the Dokies; Bility, in an editorial, questioned police brutality. The abusers of these hardworking journalists continue to parade the streets of Monrovia as if they scored a big feat. They are part of Taylor's burgeoning culture of impunity.

Still, there are dozens of other cases of mayhem going on in Liberia under the direction of the Taylor government. There is the Lofa massacre in which innocent civilians were hacked to death. There is also the case of cab driver Papa George, who was shot to death by Taylor's brother-in-law and deputy immigration commissioner, Henrique Cassell. Cassell has been "tried and convicted"; so the world is told. The reality is, as long as the Taylor administration lasts, the family of the late Papa George will never get justice. Cassell is going to live big in "prison" if he is in prison at all. In Liberia under Charles Taylor, the life of ordinary people is worth next to nothing.

Liberians, in 1997, could not have been more wrong. Taylor is not reconstructing our country with the money he reaped from the exploitation of our human and natural resources. Instead, he is using the power bestowed on him out of fear to further rip off our people, plunder what remains of our virgin forests, and isolate the country internationally. He is clamping down ruthlessly on our constitutional and human rights. In Liberia, one can no longer speak his mind without being subjected to arrest for treason. Oh, how treason has become such an overly-exploited weapon. Child Rights advocate James Torh and the Catholic priest in Buchanan are just the latest victims. Taylor has more evil up his sleeves. He, personally, epitomizes the impunity that is thriving under his direction.

Taylor means no good for Liberia. He is determined to shut the nation out from the rest of the civilized world. Star Radio, the most independent station in Monrovia, has been ransacked and shuttered. The entirety of what the outside world reads and/or hears from Liberia today emanates from the very limited coverage by the BBC and the heavily doctored reporting by the government-controlled Liberia News Agency (LINA). Liberians in the diaspora are being effectively denied the right to follow happenings in their country from an unbiased source.

In spite of all of Taylor's machinations, I still believe in the eventual liberation of Liberia, which was once upon the time, Africa's beacon of peace. We will return to a wholesome democracy whose leaders will respect the lives of the citizens. This will come through the ballot box in 2003 because Liberians will not be fooled again. Taylor has outdone himself. We will strive to ensure that this time around, people vote out of their convictions, as regards the record of the candidates and not out of fear of a self-aggrandizing warlord. No amount of pressure on the press, no amount of prejudicial killings, and no level of terror is going to beat this proud country and its people into submission come 2003.

As I intimated in a commentary in the National newspaper in 1997, *"Liberians need a president that is prepared to harmonize all dissension within our country."* We no longer have room for a mass murderer, a resource plunderer, a man that has no fear of God. As Liberians, we have a task at hand. We must wake up and save our bleeding nation. We must join forces and get Charles Taylor off our backs in 2003.

****

After an especially rough day of bad news coming out of Liberia in the fall of 1999, I sat down behind a computer in Saint John's University's library in Queens, New York to write down my thoughts on my country. This article, which was later published in the Perspective Online Magazine, was the result of that reflective moment.

A Culture of Impunity No More!

Charles Taylor, the ruffian and indicted war crimes suspect has been arrested and caged. For most of us, Liberians, there could not have been a better ending to our many years of suffering orchestrated by the Machiavellian Major Taylor. As the euphoria over this momentous arrest ebbs, we must pause to reflect on the larger significance and implications of this whole drama. What does it mean for Africa in general and, Liberia in particular? Are our leaders going to draw a lesson from this experience and get their acts together, or are they going to think this is just a happenstance and conduct business as usual?

With the culture of impunity being such an ingrained and pervasive aspect of African political power structures, it is debatable as to what many of our leaders on the continent are going to make of Taylor's reality. One thing is for sure though: the downtrodden masses of Liberia yea Africa have witnessed the dawn of a new political dispensation. We are no longer going to be fidgety about holding repressive and criminal leaders accountable for their actions and/or inactions. No more are we going to keep quiet as ruthless dictators have their way with us; we will ensure that those who commit atrocities against their own people and/or other countries' citizens face the music of their own creation. Taylor's arrest and soon-to-come trial are transformative occurrences in the history of our continent. A trend is truly taking hold in Liberia and, by extension, across Africa.

If the growing human rights activist community in Liberia and elsewhere in Africa epitomizes this trend, we have a lot to be encouraged about, and the sinister leaders have a lot to be worried about. No level of threats and intimidation will ever again stifle our resolve to out abuses perpetrated by gutless leaders. All sectors of society should now be watchdogs for responsible government. The media, most especially, must rededicate itself to its towering role as the eyes and ears of society. Actions of our political leaders must be scrutinized with the view of ensuring transparency and accountability to the people. The days of peripheral reporting on governmental activities must come to an end; media outlets must now get more investigative, even hawkish, if you will.

Going forward, Liberians, and of course, all Africans, must make concerted efforts in bringing international pressure to bear on leaders who offer blanket asylum to deposed dictators as a way of helping these buffoons evade prosecution. Hissene Habre of Chad and "Red Terror" Mengistu Haile

Mariam of Ethiopia come to mind. Wherever they are, whatever they are doing at this moment in time, make no mistake about it, they are cognizant of Taylor's reality. And, they must take it very seriously as it is only a matter of time before they too will have to answer for their crimes against humanity.

A new political order is being ushered in on the African continent, one that respects the rule of law over impunity. The nurturing of this new order should engender having murderous leaders face up to their crimes no matter how long it takes. When these hooligans begin to stare long-term incarceration, forfeiture of ill-gotten wealth, or death sentences straight in the face, they will wake up to the callous reality of their past. The expression of disbelief and fear visible on Major Taylor's face upon his handcuffing at the Robert's International Airport (RIA) said it all!

When we start to exert pressure on leaders harboring suspected war and economic crimes suspects, when we start to lobby for these keepers of suspected criminals to be charged as accessories to the crimes, we will be well on the path to stamping out impunity on our continent. Taylor's arrest is bound to change the dynamics of political leadership across Africa. Transparency is going to replace devious machinations. Like it or not, African leaders as well as ordinary folks must take serious note of the unfolding reality. That is why I was confounded when I listened to the BBC interview granted by Thelma Taylor, the rebel major's sister. In the interview, she expressed concern for her brother's safety, treatment in jail, and the propensity for an unfair trial abroad. When did these concepts become a part of the line of thought of the Taylor clan? Where was Thelma Taylor when her 'beloved brother' meted out jungle justice to the likes of the late Samuel Dokie, the late Dr. Stephen Yekeson, Counsellor Tiawon Gongloe, Activist Hassan Bility, and many others? Thelma, give me a break; your dear Major is housed in a comparatively hospitable cell, he's going to have access to a defense team; he's not going to get beaten senseless. These are the basic rights that he denied others. Stop complaining, Thelma, Liberia is on the march to accountability and your brother, Major Charles McArthur Ghankay Dakpannah Taylor is going to bear witness to this all-important transformation.

Under Charles Taylor, impunity in all of its manifestations thrived in Liberia. His arrest and upcoming trial will clear the way for sweeping institutional reforms in this and other regards. At the risk of preemption, I will emphatically state this: For Liberia, A Culture of Impunity No More! Charles Taylor is a done deal!

****

On Thursday, March 30, 2006, I was euphoric. The day before, Wednesday, March 29, 2006, Liberia's nightmare, Charles McArthur Taylor, had been arrested in Nigeria and flown to a jail cell in the Republic of Sierra Leone via the Roberts International Airport (RIA) in Liberia. This piece, published in the Online Magazine, The Perspective, chronicled my thoughts on that momentous occasion.

Liberia's Anachronistic Symbols of Division

Over three decades ago, in elementary school, I was fed half-truths, even outright inaccuracies as viable accounts of Liberian history. Notwithstanding the many years gone by since, the sting of it all makes it seem like it all happened just yesterday. Not only I'm I hurt by the blatant lies, I am equally irked that I was intentionally mis-educated! Often, I recoil when I think of how voraciously I devoured line, hook, and sinker everything I was taught from texts such as A. Doris Banks-Henries' Heroes and Heroines of Liberia and Ernest Jerome Yancy's Historical Lights of Liberia's yesterday and today.

Back then, as an utterly brainwashed child, no one could convince me, for example, that Matilda Newport was not a towering historical figure in the annals of Liberian history. My books, the only ones available to me then, told me so and my government reinforced that classroom learning with a public holiday in her honor. As I look back now, I see the folly of it all. Call me what you want but I am convinced that it is impossible, as things are today, not to be perpetually reminded of the divisive social order that has permeated Liberia ever since its independence some 161 years ago, notwithstanding the intermittent periods of awakenings (if we can call it that) we have gone through as a nation beginning with the April 1980 coup d'état.

Individual experiences, I am sure, have reeducated a great many Liberians regarding our true history. But, as the nation strives to engender trust amongst its people and promote national unity and reconciliation, a more general, government-led effort must be undertaken to correct the many inaccuracies reported in our recorded history. I'd argue that one way to start such historical cleansing is by changing our divisive national symbols. It does not augur well for us as a country to maintain symbols that are inimical to the virtues of equality, equity, and oneness of purpose. Thankfully, our present leader, President Ellen Johnson-Sirleaf has long shared this view.

On November 4, 1999 while delivering remarks at a conference on the Liberian economy at the Unity Conference Center in Monrovia, in her capacity as a leading opposition politician, she said:

> *Let us not be timid in seeking changes in the national motto, the flag, the wordings of citations of merit, and more importantly, the constitution...[and] a rewriting of our history to give due recognition to the role, lifestyle and contribution to nation building of the indigenous population.*

I am not naive as to think that my position on this issue will not draw the ire of some who will argue that at this juncture in the checkered life of our country, more pressing and substantive projects deserve much more attention than expending valuable time, effort and resources on changing national symbols. I am quite sensitive to the merits of such an argument. Indeed, I know and appreciate the enormous challenges our government face in rehabilitating our country: broken national institutions need resurrection; reconciliation is urgently needed; the nation's infrastructure needs repairs. Yes, I am aware that Liberia is in dire straits.

However, I subscribe to the school of thought which posits that all of these ills that we now suffer are rooted in a foundational cause-the endemic feeling of exclusion and inequities that has been the Achilles heel of our nation ever since its birth. That feeling of exclusion, and suppression, I might add, finds expression in our native-diminishing, if not demeaning, national symbols.

If we are going to achieve the lofty goal of solving the big problems of institutional capacity building and national reconciliation, we "must" first address those underlying issues that will serve as the basis for the equal participation of all groups of Liberians in the process. There is not a better representative such issue as altering our national symbols to reflect reverence for and equality amongst all of our people in the quest for national consensus on these so-called "big problems."

After all, did "The Love of Liberty" bring us here as our national motto suggests? Not if "us" refers to any member of the indigenous population of the country. As we all know, the touted "love of liberty" met a whole host of us here. Does the red color in the Liberian Flag represent "valor and bravery ....and the great courage" that our founders displayed in the formation of the country? Not if our "founders" refers to any indigenous participant. As is well documented, among acts that constituted the so-called valor, bravery and courage was Matilda Newport's setting off of a mortar that decimated many natives.

The watercraft portrayed on the national seal represents "the means by which our founders reached the Grain Coast from bondage in America." I do not know about you, but my ancestors never left the African shores needless to say they arrived back via a ship. Our national symbols, as can be seen from these few examples, are inaccurate, condescending, and unrepresentative of the true picture of the actions and/or interactions that obtained before, during, and after the formation of Liberia.

It behooves us as a people of conscience to work toward correcting the wrong perceptions these symbols project. That is why in 1999, I thought highly of President Ellen Johnson-Sirleaf, then a staunch opposition politician, when she courageously decried "the constraints imposed by one hundred, fifty years of power and privilege monopolization" and talked about the abhorrence of the divisive national symbols. She craved that the country would make a clean break with the past of "clinging to those anachronistic symbols of a lost and dubious glory" in favor of "walking boldly into the future, embracing the requirements of a new and fast globalizing world."

That future of which Madam President so eloquently spoke in 1999 is upon us. With the mantle of political leadership now firmly in her grasp, it is incumbent upon her to initiate the necessary legislative and other mechanisms to effect the changes. If she does, she would have lived up to her convictions as expressed in her "Framework for Change and Renewal Address" some nine years ago. If she does not, history and posterity will remember her as just another opportunist who played the people for mere political gains.

Madame President, the challenge is all yours. I hope you are up to it.

****

The case for revisiting Liberia's national symbols has been made by many including current President Ellen-Johnson-Sirleaf when she was a leading opposition politician in 1999. This article was written to express my own frustration with the lack of willpower by the powers- that-be to initiate meaningful action to correct the lies and misinformation these symbols represent.

Reflections on Liberia's March to Democracy and Prosperity

Phew! What a treacherous 14 years it was for Liberia, the warring years of 1989 through 2003 that is. Looking back now, it almost seems unreal, like a horribly scary dream from which we could not awaken. December 24, 1989, a date which, for most Liberians, "will live in infamy" to borrow the words of the late U.S. president Franklin D. Roosevelt, was when the now disgraced Charles Taylor unleashed unmitigated carnage and anarchy on our once peaceful nation. Unquestionably, the underlying factor responsible for this senseless onslaught on Liberia, as we all came to realize, was not a conscientious desire to eliminate a dictatorship, but rather a cunning ploy to amass wealth and assume unguided power.

I am in no way making a case that there were not social, economic, and political ills in Liberia that needed redress by December 24, 1989. Of course, the Doe regime, for all I know, was failing gravely on those scores. What I am driving home is the deception-the pretext of having come to save Liberia, while in reality, the self-proclaimed "freedom fighters" were harboring wicked plans to, without remorse, obliterate the manpower and natural resources of our country. This reckless pillaging was carried-out with scant regard for the indelible effects it would have not only on the present generation of Liberians, but even for those generations that were yet unborn. The brutality of Charles Taylor and his band of rowdy foot soldiers was characterized by the absence of a sense of responsibility for the destiny of our country. It was the manifestation of egocentrism to its highest order.

Today, the architect of mayhem, Mr. Taylor, sits in a prison cell in Freetown. In the spirit of democracy and justice, he will have his day in court where he will be represented by the best legal minds his ill-gotten wealth can buy. Not one to mince words let me say this: I hope he will be found guilty beyond the reasonable doubt. As we struggle to put these awful times in the history of our country behind us, there could be nothing more pleasing than having Mr. Taylor live a long and agonizing life in prison where he will perish a lonely man, a forgotten man, a tragic footnote in the annals of Liberian history.

After all that we have been through, am I proud to be a Liberian? You bet! Never will I want to be anything else. Liberians are a resilient people and it warms my heart to be a part of that tradition. We survived Charles Taylor and his evil designs. Now, we are looking forward to better days, days aglow with unity, peace, and development. The achievement of these longed-for virtues, however, requires our collective effort. As a people, we must turn our backs once and for all on greed, selfishness, primitive sentiments, prejudices, and so on. These vices must be replaced by the showing of a sense of belonging to Liberia. We must redirect our thoughts and actions at supporting our government in whatever way each of us can, in forming a consensus basis for a sustained national political, economic, social, and cultural program.

The aforementioned is not a matter of choice; it is the only way out of our quagmire. In all truth, I hold the conviction that regardless of tribe, political affiliation, or religious persuasion, Liberians share much more similarities than differences. We must exploit the opportunities we have to cooperate with each other in cultivating a glorious legacy of history, culture, and tradition for our greatest party-The Republic of Liberia. From whence we come, it is imperative that we begin to project a cohesive national identity characterized by civilized values-trust, honesty, hard work, initiative, and respect for the mutual rights of others.

In pursuing this goal, we must spurn the parochial notion that Liberia is an irreparably divided nation. We must demonstrate that we can rise above self-interests; that we can live and work to propagate political, tribal and religious tolerance and gender equity, that we are ready to resolve all aspects of dissension within our communities. We cannot, but fare admirably in this effort. Our fate as a nation truly rests on it. A big first step in this direction was accomplished when Liberians voted the way they did in the election that brought the Ellen Johnson-Sirleaf government to power. Our people must have seen the electoral process through the eyes of the late American President Abraham Lincoln, as "essentially a people's contest...a struggle for maintaining in the world that form of government whose leading objective is to elevate the condition of men ...to afford all an unfettered start, and a fair chance in the race of life". If President Johnson-Sirleaf proves me right, which I hope she will, her government will be just that.

Madame President, we are all eyes and ears, looking at and listening to you in anticipation of the great days to come.

****

This article was written in 2005 immediately following the election of President Ellen Johnson-Sirleaf to her first term of office. It was a product of both my relief at Liberia finally emerging from the dark days of civil war and my hope for a brighter, more prosperous future for the country under a new president who, as an opposition politician, had said all the right things.

On This Score, Madame President, I Beg to Differ

"You know, our country [has] been going through civil war and there were abuses. The crime rate at this time has increased. It's a tough job but somebody has to do it. I am going there now to try and bring back law and order." ---- *Beatrice Munah Sieh (March 2006).*

The above quote contains the immortal words of Beatrice Munah Sieh, the embattled Director of Police of the Republic of Liberia to ABC Action News in Trenton, New Jersey upon her preferment by the Liberian president. Those pronouncements were met with profound happiness by Liberians in many quarters. At long last, some of us hoped, our national police force was about to be headed by a principled and very well prepared leader. Ever since Colonel Sieh assumed the helm of leadership at the LNP, however, it seems she has gone completely astray of those monumental promises she made to us and the world.

Instead of 'bringing back law and order,' she is orchestrating chaos after chaos. It appears the once vaunted Director of Police has a penchant for missteps. I am beginning to wonder as to whether power has had an intoxicating effect on her. From her infamous threatening of Moslem women against wearing their religious veils which she malignly associated with terrorism, to her recent ambushing of the Seaport Police, Colonel Sieh appears determined to introduce a police state in Liberia. As our nation gradually returns to normalcy, we do not have the luxury to accommodate discordant, inept, and reckless government officials. We have way too much at stake.

To say I am disappointed in the Police Director would be an understatement. I am far past that juncture. What I am right now is scared. I fear for Liberia. I fear not because I think Colonel Sieh is single-handedly capable of derailing our march to normalcy, but because of the practice of cronyism seeping back into the governmental fabric. When the President starts to renege on her pre-election pledge to dispense her authority in the best interest of the country by paying scant attention to misconduct of certain officials, when we start to see investigative commissions set up merely for the sake of calming tensions and nothing more, we begin to fret for our fledgling democracy.

With all due respect, President Sirleaf's refusal to honor her promise to implement recommendations from the Henry Boima Fahnbulleh, Jr. commission to the letter is counterproductive at best, and downright regressive, at worst. This, I am afraid, signals the beginning of a troubling pattern of impunity reminiscent of past regimes. It brings us bitter reminders of the days in Liberia when the president's circle of men and women were practically beyond reproach. In our quest for responsible governance which we still hope President Sirleaf can spearhead, we cannot afford to stumble so early.

After putting her foot in her mouth by making insensitive statements against Liberian Muslims, after ambushing the seaport police and civilian bystanders, after coordinating aggravating utterances from the police department that diametrically contradicted the Executive Mansion's pronouncements on the issue of ammunition discovered in Gbarnga, all the Director gets is a slap on the wrist? For God sake, Madame President, how many strikes does she need to be out? She just flat out does not have the training and capacity to do the job effectively. Requiring her to train on the job, as the President has instructed, does not mitigate the damage she has caused and will continue to cause to the fragile peace we are now enjoying.

My question is: when did our government positions become internships? When we sent the butcher Charles McArthur Taylor to his life of solitude, we thought the days of putting people in positions for which they are not qualify were behind us. Nothing personal against Munah Sieh, from what I hear she was an excellent police motorbike rider during the O.A.U. summit in 1979; I also hear that she was a decent Special Education teacher in New Jersey. Those jobs, however, did not prepare her in the least for her current preferment. She is truly way in above her head. She knows not what she is doing. And that, Madame President, is a dangerous thing.

My attention has been drawn, also, to the appeal made by Lofa County Representative, Miriam K. Jalabah to the President beseeching her to spare Director Sieh the axe. What an instructive lesson in contradiction! The honorable lawmaker was elected to carve the laws and ensure that citizens regardless of their positions in society abide by them. When an official charged with enforcing the very laws begins to short-circuit them, the least we expect from Honorable Jalabah is an effort to hold such official accountable. Her call for a reprieve brings into question her understanding of her role in the governmental structure. The honorable representative argues, "We all have made mistakes one way or the other but for the sake of peace, we must also be prepared to forgive others." I counter that it is precisely for the sake of maintaining our fragile peace that a divisive and ill-prepared official like Director Sieh must be let go.

The Fahbulleh commission, after investigating the Freeport melee, saw exactly what I'm seeing. They found Director Sieh as being the most responsible for what transpired Based on her level of culpability they recommended that she be relieved of her post. President Sirleaf decided to give her a reprieve instead. I think that was an error in the use of discretionary power. On that score, Madame President, I beg to respectfully differ with your line of reasoning.

****

When Munah Sieh was plucked out of obscurity from a New Jersey, U.S.A. public school classroom and appointed to the post of Liberia's Director of Police, I was ecstatic. I thought it was a good thing that the country would have a female officer of integrity heading the police force. It turned out my hopes would be dashed in short order. Director Sieh became notorious for egregious missteps. For quite a long time, the president gave her mere slaps on the wrist for her numerous transgressions. This article was written in protest of the President's strategy in dealing with the Director's shortcomings.

The Law Must Prevail Over Expediency I

Over the years, I have followed with admiration and respect Mr. Arthur Dennis' commentaries on issues pivotal to Liberia's growth and development as a democracy. More often than not, in my humble opinion, he has been on the mark with his instructive analyses. However, on the issue of the recent presidential appointment of a mayor, an elective post per legislative enactment, he dropped the ball. For him to conclude that President Ellen Johnson-Sirleaf was not in contravention of the laws of the land when she appointed Ms. Betty Breeze- Doe as Mayor of Zwedru City confounds me.

Not only were his analogies regarding seeming precedents in the United States and Liberia totally out of place, his historical notes as well, did absolutely nothing to pinpoint why he believes it is not a violation of the constitution for the president to fill elective offices with appointed officials. In his piece, Mr. Dennis argued that "there is absolutely no provision under the constitution, prohibiting the President from appointing elected officials." He went on to cite the following in support of his claim: "In 1998, President Charles Taylor nominated Senator

Eddington A. Varmah from the Senate and appointed him to serve as Minister of Justice. In 2002, President George Bush nominated Porter J. Goss from the U.S. House of Representatives and appointed him to serve as CIA Director."

Yes, Mr. Dennis, it is absolutely within the purview of the president to appoint elected officials to "appointive positions" so long as the "elected officials" vacate their elective offices upon their own volition. However, it is one thing to appoint elected officials to "appointive positions" and quite another thing for the president to appoint people to "elective positions". So, while President Bush appointed Congressman Porter Goss to the CIA post and the ruffian Taylor appointed Senator Eddington Varmah as Minister, it is unthinkable that either president would have appointed someone to an elective post such as senator, mayor, representative, and so on. That would be a breach of the laws.

Let us not forget, Mr. Dennis, that an Act passed by the National Legislature on August 9, 1979 makes the position of City Mayor in Liberia an elective post. Specifically, the Act stipulates that mayoral elections shall be held on the second Tuesday in November after every four years. This law is unambiguous and leaves no room for such interpretation as "the appointment of City Mayors and the elections [sic] of City Mayors are consistent with laws" as your article would lead us to believe. As far as I know, the 1986 constitution did not abrogate this law in any way, shape or form. Establishing this premise as a point of departure, it seems to me, Mr. Dennis, that the other point you stressed that "at this period of our national reconstruction program, US$32 million is a lot of money that can be used to rebuild the Tubman Bridge or renovate more roads for citizens and their goods to move freely in the country" becomes moot. While the rebuilding of the nation's infrastructure is important, it must not be carried out at the expense of the very foundation that makes it possible in the first place. We all know it was extremely expensive to organize and execute the elections that brought President Sirleaf to power, but it had to be done because as a country we needed to begin our journey of reconstruction on the right footing-with the tenets of democracy and good governance.

If we let the physical reconstruction demands to undermine official adherence to the provisions of the constitution and/or legislative enactments , we will be setting ourselves up for yet another round of trouble times. As we work to revive our country, we must do so bearing in mind that responsible governance is the first key to success. And, respect for and adherence to the laws by our leaders is the starting point of that process.

Sir, your argument to the effect that the criteria for city status be revisited has merit. I could not agree with you more that since most of the approximately 500 cities in Liberia are really just tiny towns, it is foolhardy of us as a nation to continue to expend huge sums to conduct mayoral elections in these locales. If such proposal was channeled through the legislature and the appropriate debates are held and laws enacted to effect these changes, it would solve once and for all the issue of unnecessary expenditures. Even more important, that would be democracy at work. And that, sir, will be the best way forward.

Outside of enacting laws to quash undeserving cities, and in the absence of legislative enactments designating the post of mayor as an appointive office, the president will do well to restrain her desire to appoint mayors. Our constitution limits her appointment power to certain offices (see Article 54). Making appointments to positions, which by legislative enactment, are subject to elections, is a breach of the laws, and by extension, a violation of the constitution. There are neither ifs nor buts about that.

****

Colonel Arthur Dennis (rtd.), a former Liberian military brass and former high ranking functionary at both the Ministries of Information and Defense and I disagreed on the constitutionality of President Ellen Johnson-Sirleaf appointment of Ms. Betty Breeze to the 'elective' post of City Mayor of Zwedru City, Grand Gedeh County. This was my initial piece to express my respectful disagreement with Colonel Dennis.

The Law Must Prevail Over Expediency II

In a scathing rejoinder to my counter to his article titled "*City Mayors Should Be Appointed, Not Elected*" published by The Analyst online magazine recently, Mr. Arthur Dennis accuses me of, among other things: not understanding the dynamic nature of laws, favoring expensive elections over the people's immediate welfare, grossly misquoting the critical issues contained in his article, and taking his whole message out of context. Further, Mr. Dennis challenged me to highlight the particular paragraph in which he absolved the president of violation of the laws by her appointment of Ms. Betty Breeze as Zwedru City Mayor. If I am unable to do so, Mr. Dennis retorts, "an apology for intellectual dishonesty" would be deserved. Fair enough.

In answer, I will start from where I ended my article that prompted Mr. Dennis' ire. Here is what I wrote in my concluding comments:

> *Making appointments to positions, which by legislative enactment, are subject to elections, is a breach of the laws, and by extension, a violation of the*

constitution. There are neither ifs nor buts about that.

This assertion continues to be the basis upon which I will now take up the challenge to prove that indeed, Mr. Dennis, in his article, insinuated that President Ellen Johnson-Sirleaf did not violate the law by appointing Ms. Breeze as City Mayor, an elective office.

First, let me remind Mr. Dennis that I need not be reeducated (through extensive and unnecessary lectures as regards Aristotle, Cero, Locke, Roosevelt, et al) that laws are not meant to be static. And, for the record, I am not an advocate of rigid adherence to expending much needed funds on conducting nationwide mayoral elections over more urgent needs of the public as Mr. Dennis suggests. I know and value the dynamic nature of laws. But here is where I think differently: I believe that dynamism of the law does not preclude observance of procedural safeguards for orderly repeals. Therefore, if laws must be changed to reflect changing times and circumstances, the changes must be channeled through the constitutionally mandated framework of the legislative process. When the president attempts to circumvent this process by appointing personnel to serve in elective posts, no one must assail me for crying out loud. For to do otherwise, will be a disservice to my country. So, if Mr. Dennis subscribes to the view that in "the interest of the public good" the president can break the law, then I will respectfully beg to differ.

Had Mr. Dennis read my article a little more thoroughly, and, with less of an emotional bent, he would have noticed that I gave him kudos for the ideas he espoused regarding revisiting the issue of too many undeserving cities in Liberia. I thought his proposal to switch from electing mayors to having a city council appoint a city manager was appropriate. Here is what I specifically wrote in that regard:

> *I could not agree with you more that since most of the approximately 500 cities in Liberia are really just tiny towns, it is foolhardy of us as a nation to continue to expend huge sums to conduct mayoral elections in these locales. If such proposal was channeled through the legislature and the appropriate debates are held and laws enacted to effect these changes, it would solve once and for all the issue of unnecessary expenditures. Even more important, that would be democracy at work. And that, sir, will be the best way forward.*

How much more succinct could I be on this question? So, you see, I'm not a proponent of sticking with laws that have outlived their relevance insofar as not keeping pace with the public's interest. What I am, instead, is a stickler for adhering to the procedural constitutional process of repealing such irrelevant laws. Hijacking the process, as the president tried to do, is unacceptable.

Second, Mr. Dennis launches into a hypothetical to justify his call for the diversion of funds from the Elections Commission in favor of infrastructural projects. In so doing, he employs a broad brush to paint me as someone who does not care about the people's welfare. Here is what he wrote:

> *Whenever public interest takes precedence over any law in a peculiar situation, as Locke said, the executive should use discretionary powers to preserve public interest. For example, what if Liberians in the diasporas wake up one morning in surprise and here [sic] news that starvation has hit Liberia; hundreds of people are dying daily from hunger and hunger-related diseases. The government of Liberia has US$32*

million reserved in the bank for mayoral elections. The President has two proposals on the table. One proposal calls on government to use the money and buy food for the starving population; and the other calls on government to hold mayoral elections in the wake of the starvation. Professor Dudu, what factor takes precedence in this crisis, and which proposal would you support?

I hurry to remind Mr. Dennis that our government should not, and does not operate on 'what ifs.' The government has a budget bureau, which, based on consultations with the various ministries and autonomous agencies, makes budgetary allocations for all aspects of the government's operation. So, funds are not just arbitrarily moved around from one budgetary allotment to another using the "discretionary power" of the president. It takes much more than that, sir.

The question, therefore, should not be if I will support the expending of US$32 million for holding mayoral elections over feeding a starving population. Rather, it should be whether I support strategic budgetary allocations as opposed to impromptu disbursements using the president's discretion. If this were the question, my answer would be a resounding YES. Until and unless there is an emergency in the country that demands such a radical shift from budgetary appropriations, your hypothetical situation is irrelevant to the discussion at hand. In a democracy, mind you, even emergency powers are not seized, they are granted by provisions of law.

I prefer, therefore, that we dwell on realities. When we allow our president to operate outside of the parameters of budgetary accountability, we are in effect giving her a blank check to do as she wishes with the public coffers. That, my friend, will be a grim commentary on our readiness to embrace the principles of good governance.

Third, I did not deliberately misquote the critical issues in Mr. Dennis' article. Here is one assertion he made:

> *There is absolutely no provision under the constitution, prohibiting the President from appointing elected officials. In 1998, President Charles Tqylor nominated Senator Eddington A. Varmah from the Senate and appointed him to serve as Minister of Justice. In 2002, President George Bush nominated Porter J. Goss from the U.S. House of Representatives and*

appointed him to serve as CIA Director. Therefore, if President Johnson-Sirleaf chooses to appoint City Mayors or other elected officials to positions under the executive branch, she is duly protected under the constitution, and she will win the argument in case the matter goes to court.

I must say this was pretty confounding as the issue under discussion was not about the president appointing an elected official. Rather, the issue was the president's ill-advised appointment of Ms. Breeze to an elective office. So, I was left to ponder what Mr. Dennis' analogies were meant to imply vis-a-vis the president's action. That President Sirleaf was in the right to appoint a City Mayor? If so, then what is his bone of contention regarding misquotation and/or contextual misrepresentation? On the other hand, if by these references, Mr. Dennis meant to espouse the president's right to appoint elected officials to appointive offices, then I will remind him that that was not the issue on the table. No one is challenging that right. Not me, not the opposition parties.

Therefore, outside of the possibility that the above quote confused the prevailing issues, I do not see the point it tried to make relative to the president's audacity to appoint Ms. Breeze. If Mr. Dennis argues that he was writing in total isolation of the Zwedru incident, then what use was his reference to the president winning "the argument in case the matter goes to court"? Which matter is going to court? The only matter that went to court, as far as I know, was the President's attempt to torpedo the law by appointing a City Mayor. The Supreme Court issued an injunction effectively barring her from breaking the law. She was not vindicated. She was ordered to forthwith cease her attempt at usurping legislative authority — short-circuiting the process of repealing a law.

So, the issue was less about me misquoting, and more about Mr. Dennis snowballing us with information that were basically fillers-having nothing whatsoever to do with the crux of the issue under consideration. If in the process, therefore, Mr. Dennis feels there were contextual misrepresentations of his intended message, it may have been as a result of the level of ambiguity contained in the message. While the case in point was about the president's authority as regards appointments to elective offices, his analogies were about the president's power to appoint elected officials to appointive posts — an authority that was not being challenged by anybody, in anyway.

So, do I apologize to Mr. Dennis? Well, on the score of his accusations, I would think not. But then again, I respect our Liberian tradition — the elders are always in the right. By that token, I'd say "never mind yah" for any lingering hurt that may have resulted from my review of your article and its inherent analysis. And, you may have the last word on this issue, if you so desire.

****

After Colonel Dennis responded to my initial article with a rather scathing rebuttal, I wrote this counter to clarify and reinforce certain points. The Colonel, whom I respect and admire fervently for his intellectual wits, and I, via private e-mail exchanges, buried the hatchet and agreed that ours was a healthy debate and we moved on.

Chief Justice's Outburst, Much Ado about Nothing

It is deeply troubling that the Chief Justice of the Republic of Liberia, the nation's top legal guru, has fallen prey to the ill-conceived trend of official power intoxication. With a litany of threats aimed at the "free" media in Liberia, His Honor, Johnnie N. Lewis is attempting to reinstitute the putrid culture of harassment against the press. Liberians both at home and in the Diaspora have not forgotten the days in the not-too-distant past when media houses were razed to the ground, journalists flogged, and some even killed. Those were awful, chilling, and regrettable times in the annals of Liberian history. And, there is no way we are going to let that part of our history repeat itself ever. That is why we must speak up now as silence in times like these is tantamount to tacit acquiescence.

No, I do not condone willful ineptitude on the part of media practitioners. In fact, journalists, I believe, must strive for the requisite education, training, and experience necessary to execute the functions of their sacred role, especially in a democracy as young as ours. The professional obligation to report truthful and balanced news stories must be adhered to at all times no matter what.

In the process of piquing the public's interest in national dialogue and deliberative democracy, journalists must never compromise the veracity of content.

I will have no problem with reprimands for journalists who violate these substantive tenets of the profession so long as said reprimands are done within the framework of legality. However, for the Chief Justice to go ballistic over such cosmetic issues as certain members of the media "giving him wrong and inappropriate titles, misspelling his name, and attaching his photo to stories that have nothing to do with him" is beyond reason. Taking time off from the people's work to invite several heads of media houses to the Supreme Court chambers to issue "last chance, 30-day jail" threats over triviality is unacceptable.

In these transitional times, our Chief Justice should be more concerned about addressing the burning issue of the broken legal system within the country. As at this writing, there is no functioning legal apparatus in most political subdivisions of the nation. Preoccupation with titles, and spelling of his name, at least to me, borders on a sort of perverse obsession with the superficial trappings of the government position he holds. Doesn't the Supreme Court docket have cases that require redress at this time? The time the Chief Justice takes to assume the role of Liberia's "chief spelling instructor," supplying journalists with plain paper and dictating his proper title and the correct spelling of his name should be spent framing legal opinions that future generations of legal scholars will someday reference. That is what he is paid to do.

I am disappointed in Justice Lewis's antics. His outburst was much ado about nothing. My hope is that the courageous men and women in the Liberian media will not be cowered by these threats. Our country has endured too much for way too long. You cannot surrender now. You must continue to do your job with ruthless efficiency.

****

When Chief Justice Johnny Lewis-by most accounts a very capable jurist in his heydays-began experiencing, apparently, the ill-effects of aging and its accompanying health drawbacks, he started to demonstrate a clearly erratic behavior pattern. This commentary was written in response to his infamous outburst about journalists "giving him inappropriate titles and misspelling his name."

Of Power, Privilege, and Justice

The mix of power, privilege and justice can sometimes be harmful. In many instances, those upon whom power and privilege are bestowed are ill-prepared to exercise them prudently. For such people, these societal bequests are potent intoxicants that blind them to the necessity of justice as it concerns the less powerful, the less privileged. The reality of this narrative is enhanced by my experiences here in the United States of America and back home in Africa. It is even more pronounced in my dear country, Liberia. This is especially so when we examine the subject in the context of the abuse of official power and privilege in our national political structures.

This essay, sets out to indict neither any one person nor group as a poster child of this transgression; rather, it seeks to examine the negative impact the practice has on the virtues of morality, accountability, fairness, and, of course, jurisprudence in our country. And to that extent, sound a clarion call for our leaders to pay special attention to both the subtle and evident manners in which the practice is carried-out.

Harmonizing power, privilege, and justice presents a challenging landscape, one fraught with political, social, economic, and cultural minefields. It is no secret that in any given society, "who gets what and why?" as the American sociologist Gerhart Lenski framed it in his study of social stratification, pits competing interests against each other. This interplay culminates into the exertion of undue influences that are direct functions of power and privilege to the utter detriment of juridical tenets. Such unmitigated exercise of power and privilege as ultimate trump cards to gain advantageous footholds in society breeds a dichotomous depiction of two classes with deep-seated differences. In other words, it creates a society of 'haves and have-nots.' This in turn morphs into the perfect conditions for conflicts as we have had in Liberia and other parts of Africa.

If we have learned anything at all from our country and continent's history of unending conflicts, it should be the maxim that "granting individuals or groups special status, with special rights, distinct from the majority of the people, means that the majority will suffer discrimination." That the majority will fight back, of course, is a foregone conclusion. Have we really learned this fact? Let's find out. My much-loved Liberia presents a classic example of how not to employ power and privilege. I say so because it is one country where class structures have permeated every single day of our existence. From 1847 to 1980, the Americo-Liberian oligarchy thrived on power and privilege to cow and rule the indigenous population with scant regard for justice in any way, shape, or form. Whether it was who got what job or who got favorable judicial rulings or who got scholarships to study overseas, it was all decided principally on the basis of the social class to which people belonged. What a sad commentary to recall.

Then came April 12, 1980 when the decadent oligarchy was overthrown by a military junta composed almost entirely of indigenous tribesmen. As people danced in the streets of Monrovia on that day, little did they realize that sadly enough, the culture of a dichotomous social stratum would not change under this regime. And that in fact, patronage and its perilous appendages would take on an added urgency and a renewed sense of significance. Any wonder then why our country imploded soonest the gluttonous Charles Taylor tapped into our seething discontent with the impiety of social stratification? No one has put this depressing state of affairs we suffered in a more succinct and compelling perspective any better than our learned President Ellen Johnson-Sirleaf. Referencing April 12, 1980 in a paper titled "Liberia: A Framework for Change and Renewal" delivered in 1999, she aptly said:

> *The constraints imposed by one hundred, fifty years of power and privilege monopolization were broken, providing*

the basis for a fundamental altering of the framework of economic, political and social systems that had been shaped over those many years of settler domination. It did not happen. It did not happen because the new political leaders, born, bred, and imbued with the value system of the past lacked the capacity to formulate a new vision for a country long in need to move away from its past. It did not happen because the intellectual support group, upon which these new leaders relied, lacked themselves the reformist qualities necessary to modernize the nation. And so we witnessed a transfer of the trappings of a fallen oligarchy; we settled for a mere shifting of the monopolization of power and privilege from one group to another — yes, to another group long denied, and hence deserving, but by its embrace of the status quo, the new rulers set the stage for where we are today — not much further than where we were some fifty years ago — by international standards, a thoroughly backward nation — economically, socially and politically.

What eloquence! The president was on the money here. Now, it has been nearly a decade since Madam Johnson-Sirleaf delivered this insightful paper. Yet, we continue to witness a burgeoning culture of injudicious exercise of power and privilege in Liberia. We continue to see with consternation, individuals and perhaps, groups that still enjoy a set of advantages and/or immunities beyond those common to all others.

For example, why during a prison transfer, was Senator Roland Kaine, under arrest for alleged capital murder, able to walk without handcuffs, bottled water and cellular phone in hand, chatting up members of the media while the 'common guys', his fellow accused, were shackled? Was it due to the power and privilege conferred on him by his position in Liberian society? Why was Police Director Munah Sieh — after committing one too many times, offenses that would have landed any ordinary Liberian in trouble, even prison- given a free pass? For the record, the police chief issued public statements that went afoul of the Executive Mansion's account of a national security case involving a cache of ammunition; she made outrageous, inflammatory, divisive, and even threatening remarks against Muslim women who, in deference to their religious beliefs, wore veils in public. To cap all of that off, she was judged the most culpable (by the H. Boima Fahnbulleh, Jr. led commission) for instigating the ambush of the Seaport Police. This action resulted in bodily harm to scores of people including innocent bystanders. For all of these transgressions, and in the face of the Fahnbulleh Commission's unequivocal recommendation for her to be relieved of her post, the powerful and privileged Director was instead given a slap on the wrist — ordered to take some leadership classes.

I would think that for these same offenses, an ordinary Liberian would have been at the notorious South Beach Prison today possibly awaiting prosecution. Don't you agree? While these examples may be insufficient as a basis for questioning the president's convictions on the misuse of power and privilege as expressed in her 1999 paper, they sure raised some eyebrows. Owing to that, I strongly call on the president to demonstrate vigilance in wresting this abhorrent practice from our national scene. I do not doubt for a second that the "Iron Lady" is capable of stepping up to the plate as the enforcer extraordinaire in this regard.

Do not get me wrong. I understand that no matter what we do as human beings, power and privilege will never be bestowed on us all equally and/or equitably. I am all too aware that economic, political, social and cultural powers and privileges are more often than not, functions of variables such as education, abilities, and lineage — variables that are beyond individual control. However, those who hold power and privilege as a result of these bequests must use them judiciously. They must employ them to bolster, not vanquish the tenets of justice. If they choose the latter option, then the appropriate arms of government must ensure that "Justice is done to all men."

I am all the more hopeful because we now have someone at the helm of government who a decade ago, realized that in the midst of all the shortcomings we have experienced as a nation, "we owe it to the thousands whose life have been lost in the struggle for change to make a choice that is right, to leave behind a legacy of which we can be proud." I know that Madame President knows that part of that legacy she so intuitively spoke of then, is ditching the entrenched Liberian culture of "you know who I am?" once and for all. I hope this is not too much to ask.

****

This commentary was written on one especially cold Winter Day in Minnesota. I was sitting at my computer in my basement with not much else to do. In such solitary moments, Liberia, of course, is the primary topic my mind naturally drifts to. On this day, I thought to reflect on the ills of identity politics.

Anti-Corruption Drive vs. Respect for the Rule of Law I

For the recently ushered in Ellen Johnson-Sirleaf government, bringing Mr. Charles Taylor to book, as rapidly as it was done, was nothing short of a watershed event. Truth be told, I was one among the many who had doubts about the resolve of the new president to act so resolutely so soon. I was dead wrong! By pressing for justice over expedience in the Charles Taylor case, President Johnson -Sirleaf has set the tone for a responsible administration. She could have taken the easy way out by first attending to what has now become known as the *more pressing issues*: providing pipe-borne water, electricity, healthcare-delivery mechanisms, education, etc. Instead, she chose to be prudent and act in the nation's long-term interest by doing away with the Taylor issue, which, had it been left to linger, threatened to cast a long shadow over whatever else she would have accomplished.

Taking off from this vantage point, it is envisaged that the president will remain strong-willed in instituting the necessary reforms that will turn Liberia toward the path of socio- economic progress. That is very much the mandate so overwhelmingly given to her by the Liberian masses. After having virtually been to hell and back in the last two and half decades of our national existence (starting from the Samuel Doe era to the maiming Charles Taylor years), Liberians have robustly broken loose from all sorts of servitude, and have wielded enormous political clout and ingenuity by electing, this time, a leadership on the substantive basis of qualification rather than on the basis of popularity or apprehension. We cannot ask anything more of our people, at least, not just yet. The challenge now falls to President Johnson-Sirleaf and her government to do their part: instituting sweeping anti-corruption reforms, ensuring national security, promoting human and infrastructure development all of which must be strategically balanced against the respect for the organic laws of the land.

This is a somewhat difficult but necessary condition to forge the burgeoning democracy that we expect to see flourish in Liberia. The administration must balance its zest to wipe out corruption with the respect for due process as called for by our constitution. Anything short of this will not only taint the achievements of the government, but will as well, defeat the purpose for which Liberians so unselfishly voted for the President. I am not pointing accusing fingers at the very young government, at least not yet. What I am pointing out is that the administration must lawfully go about the business of cleaning up the rotten culture of insurrections and corruption from the fabric of Liberia's nationhood.

Recent reports of arrests and searches without warrants in Monrovia are disturbing. Alleged mass firings at the Ministry of Defense and the Bureau of Immigration without first exhausting the necessary mechanisms laid down in the labor laws of the country deserve our attention. If there are any merits to these reports, President Johnson-Sirleaf must act to ensure that such telltale signs of abuse of power will not be allowed to fester. Our government's ability to take anti-corruption and anti-- insurrection initiatives on the one hand, and the respect for the laws of the land on the other, as interwoven issues that should be used to complement and reinforce each other while not allowing neither to down play the other is pivotal to the development of our democratic institutions.

I am impressed by the charm, charisma, and the lengthy educational and experiential track record of President Johnson-Sirleaf. I wish her nothing but the utmost best as she attempts to steer our country out of the turbulent waters of war and defilement to development and respectability. Something deep within tells me she is up to the task at hand. I cannot, therefore, be asking too much of her. In fact, the seeming pressure for this administration to deliver on its political and development agenda should not be overwhelming, not at all.

There is resounding impetus in favor of the Johnson-Sirleaf government. The international community is anxious to assist based on the president's credibility and steadfast determination to succeed at her job. The Liberian intelligentsia and technocrats are in her corner as well. Take Dr. J. Christopher Toe, for example, who left his University Presidency in the United States of America to serve in the Johnson-Sirleaf government as Agriculture Minister. This speaks volumes of the respect the President enjoys in both local and international circles. Exploiting this huge network of internal and external assets in her continuous bid to foster the cause of the Liberian populace will be the telling confirmation of her natural acumen for political leadership.

True, my demands are not a cakewalk. Liberia is in a deep muddle. As a matter of fact, we are attempting to climb out of an abyss. For the last three decades, almost all Liberian children have been born into an environment lacking opportunities and threatened by war and its attendant menaces. But that is why providence gave us President Ellen Johnson-Sirleaf. Madame President, we look to you to cultivate within our national psyche the ideal that selfless determination pursued in the just cause of personal convictions and national concerns can uproot even the most formidable barrier to social justice and sustainable human development. When you lead us in nurturing these values into a unique and forceful campaign, we will, together, succeed in lifting our beleaguered country out of the ashes of deprivation-devoid of insurrections and corruption and filled with the undying respect for the rule of law.

****

In 2006, not long after President Sirleaf had been inaugurated for her first term, reports of mass firings and unwarranted searches at the Ministry of National Defense and Bureau of Immigration filtered out of Liberia. I wrote this article in response thereof.

Anti-Corruption Drive vs. Respect for the Rule of Law II

Often, I have written about my unreserved enthusiasm and support for President Ellen Johnson-Sirleaf's public commitment to the fight against corruption. Like the President, I subscribe to the belief that to move forward as a nation, corruption-specifically the misapplication of public funds must be fought tooth and nail. In doing so, however, I have stressed that due process must be observed at all times. If we truly envisage a transparent system of governance in Liberia, it is imperative that we pursue anti-corruption initiatives lawfully. Fighting corruption and respecting the rule of law, in my view, are complementary of each other. Together, they promote responsibility and accountability in government at all levels On the other hand, if we allow our zest for eradicating corruption to short-circuit our commitment to due process, we will be headed in a perilous direction.

The online magazine, *The Analyst*, recently ran two stories that prompted the writing of this commentary. One was regarding the summary dismissal of four employees at the Ministry of Transport for what Minister Jeremiah Sulunteh described as "setting up road blocks at 15-gate in Margibi county and conducting vehicle inspection exercise without any authorization." The other story had to do with "financial malpractices, fraud and improprieties" at the finance section of the Liberia National Police (LNP).

In each of these alleged corruption cases, according to *The Analyst*, steps have been taken to enforce President's Sirleaf's inaugural pledge to "fight corruption to its core" having declared the menace as public enemy #1. It is encouraging to see that efforts are being exerted by the leaderships at both the Ministry of Transport and the Liberia National Police to address these alleged corrupt practices by some of their personnel. At the same time, it is critical to point out what I see as shortcomings and/ or inadequacies in these corruption fighting initiatives as approached at these institutions.

The Case at MOT

The Analyst reports that the dismissed employees at the Ministry of Transport "Inspectors Christine Cooper, Ralph Jacobs and William Swen, have admitted to the act of removing license plates of vehicles and extort [ing] money from vehicle owners and drivers. The Director of the Shipping Division, Jerome Julius was also dismissed for allegedly converting more than US$2, 000.00 to his personal use.

This amount, authorities disclosed, was intended for traveling allowance and ticket. They said the acts allegedly committed by the dismissed employees are in violation of Chapter 4, 2.24 of the Standing Orders for the Civil Service of Liberia."

The Analyst's story also reports the suspension of the Deputy Director responsible for Land and Road Transport, Mr. William Gaye, for one month without pay for what Minister Sulunteh called "receiving and concealing information relating to the [fraudulent] acts of the inspectors."

Shortcomings in MOT's Approach

I do not, for a second, doubt that the Minister of Transport is well-intentioned in his approach to curbing corrupt practices at his institution. But, I do have my concerns. In the quest to send a stern signal of his intolerance for corruption, Minister Sulunteh sidestepped the accused employees' rights to due process. Under the laws of Liberia, internal investigations, like the one conducted by officials at the Ministry are not sufficient grounds for the outright dismissal of the employees. We have got to remember that employees at the Ministry do not serve at the will and pleasure of the Minister. They were vetted and recruited by the Ministry of Transport and are entitled to certain protections against such dismissal actions.

Further, summary dismissal in of itself, to me, is neither sufficient punishment for the crime the employees are accused of committing nor is it an adequate enough deterrent against corruption. As the Honorable Minister contemplated his action, I wish he had consider the fact that there is a fine line between enforcing an aggressive anti-corruption drive and allowing each and every employee involved in the scandal due process. My view is that the Minister, after the internal investigation, should have suspended the accused employees pending the outcome of a trial in a court of law. If he truly believed in the strength of the evidence gathered against the employees during the internal probe, the matter should have been forwarded to the Justice Ministry for prosecution. Acting otherwise is, regardless of intent, a disservice to the very fight against corruption. After all, undermining due process is itself, corruption.

The accused employees are entitled to due process with all the constitutional rights appertaining thereto. They should be availed of the opportunity to be represented by competent legal counsel. Losing their jobs-probably their only source of income and livelihood-solely on the outcome of an internal investigation is a violation of their rights as guaranteed under our laws. The questions that come to mind include: were the alleged "confessions" that were extracted from these employees coerced? Were the employees actually acting on the authorization of a higher up in the ministry who has now hung them up to dry? Why are some supposedly complicit employees being suspended while others are getting axed? There is no way we can objectively answer these questions short of the case going to court. So, I suggest in this public manner, that Minister Sulunteh retracts his dismissal of these employees and grant them their day in court.

Maybe, just maybe, these employees, with the assistance of competent legal representation, will be able to prove, after all, that they had authorization to carry out the actions for which they are now being sacked. If that turns out to be the case, the Minister will be obliged, by law, to give them back their jobs and restore, at least in some measure, their impugned reputations. Conversely, if the employees are found guilty of committing the crimes that the Minister outlined in his dismissal letters, he could then enforce their firing. In doing so, the Minister will not only be fighting corruption but will also be exercising the required respect for due process. Moreover, the convicted employees will pay for their crimes to the fullest extent of the law. If they are guilty, dismissal alone does not punish them enough, by my reckoning. Fines, restitutions, and prison terms, as spelt out under the laws of the land will be in order.

The Case at the LNP

The Analyst quotes documents in its possession to the effect that on August 27, 2007, authorities at the Liberia National Police "were alerted to [a] wide range of financial malpractices at the Finance Section by a former staff member of the department." The paper revealed that the amount involved in the alleged financial scandal was well in excess of US$100,000.00. According to the report, the Chief of Finance at the LNP, N. Melvin Togba is the central figure in this alleged corrupt activity. The scheme, it is alleged, entailed adding ghost names to the LNP payroll, clandestinely extracting paychecks that belonged to other active members of the force, and cashing those checks and converting the proceeds to personal use.

"Due to the weight of the allegations," *The Analyst reports*, Police Inspector General Munah Sieh "constituted an investigative commission to probe the authenticity of the matter." At the end of its work, the commission "established and confirmed that N. Melvin Togba, Chief of Finance and his corps of officers within the Department were engaged in acts unbecoming of professional police officers." Further, according to *The Analyst*, the commission "found that the names placed on the Liberian National Police (LNP) payroll by Superintendent Massa Bestman-Ezumah were not of any active police officers; terming it as complete fraud and an attempt to deceive and misrepresent the administration of the LNP." These actions, the Commission concluded, "contravenes Article III, Section 1, Page 13 of the National Police Duty Manual under the caption: Involvement of Police Officers in Criminal and Related Offences," as well as Section 15.51, "Theft of Property" under the New Penal Law of Liberia."

As a result, the commission recommended "the transfer of N. Melvin Togba from the Finance Section as well as his suspension off-the-job for the period of three months with appropriate salary deduction." For Superintendent Bestman-Ezuman, the commission recommended that she "be transferred from the Department of Finance, suspended for 2 months with the same measure of salary reduction" as her boss.

Shortcomings in the LNP's Approach

It would be unfair were I to say that there are shortcomings and/or inadequacies with the way in which Inspector General Sieh has handled this corruption scandal so far. From *The Analyst's* report, it is not known if the Inspector has endorsed and/ or implemented the investigative commission's recommendations. She was absolutely correct to appoint the investigative commission as a first step toward remedying the problem. The inadequacies, therefore, lie in the recommendations made by the investigative commission. It is incomprehensible for the commission to be recommending transfers and one to two month suspensions as remedies for gross misapplication of public funds to the tone of over US$100,000 .00. In my view, in addition to the suspensions, the commission's recommendations should have included wording to the effect that the accused Finance Department officials be forwarded to the ministry of justice for prosecution. I am left at sea as to the motivations that underpin the commission's "slap on the wrist" recommendations for such serious alleged financial improprieties. Do the Commission members live in the proverbial "glass house" and therefore, are not willing to cast stones? I do not wish to sound accusatory here but it is hard not to in the face of these laughable recommendations.

At the end of a year in which Inspector General Munah Sieh has been embroiled in some questionable situations that had many including this writer questioning her fitness for office, she now has a chance to begin to redeem herself. Yes, the ball now falls squarely into her lap as I, and hopefully everyone else that has a vested interest in the fight against corruption and the promotion of the rule of law in Liberia, look to see whether or not she will endorse and implement these recommendations as they are. If I were a betting guy, I would bet that she will go one step further by forwarding this case to the ministry of

Justice for prosecution. If the officers are exonerated based on adduced evidence, she should move to reinstate them promptly. On the other hand, if they are found guilty beyond the reasonable doubt, she must move swiftly to dishonorably discharge them from the police force. The rest will be left to the court system to ensure, under appropriate sentencing guidelines, that the "guilty" officers pay the requisite fines, restitutions, and serve prison sentences as prescribed by law.

Conclusion

Corruption, like our president says, is "Liberia's Public Enemy # 1." There is no denying this fact. Purging this menace from every level of our government and private sector is an effort worthy of our fullest support. It is important, however, to remain ever cognizant of the necessity to temper our aggressive anti-- corruption initiatives with a whole-hearted commitment to the rule of law. This way, we will ensure that we do not heal one wound by opening another ghastly one. The manner in which the referenced cases at the Ministry of Transport and the Liberia National Police are being handled, at least to this point, leaves a lot to be desired. It is my hope that the Ministry of Labor and the Ministry of Justice will wake up to the realities that these sample cases reflect. In concert with other agencies, they must work to correct these glaring inadequacies. Where civil servants are being railroaded, the Ministry of Labor must step in to protect their rights under the labor laws. In the cases where massive corruption scandals are being treated like child's play, the Justice Ministry must exert its authority to enforce the penal code. Such is the delicate balance that is required if the President's proclaimed crusade against corruption is going to succeed.

After all is said and done, Liberia must remain a country of laws, not of men.

****

This article was written in continuation of efforts to highlight incidents of the lack of respect for the rule of law in the "fight" against corruption. Cases at the Liberia National Police (LNP) and the Ministry of Transport (MOT) were examined.

The TPS Dilemma: A Case for Ending the Cycle of Yearly Reprieves

On the cusp of summary expulsion from the United States yet again, thousands of Liberians are about to be granted another 12- month reprieve. H.R 3123, the U.S. House of Representatives' bill calling for this stay of action is a laudable initiative. Sadly, however, it does not address the issue of permanency in status for our people. Since 1990, when the scourge of war drove many of us to these United States, it has been our hope that the government here would see reason to regularize the status of the many Liberians that are now an ingrained part of this country, toiling daily to eke out an honest living as law-abiding and tax- paying residents. This, obviously, has not been the case. The U.S. authorities have been reluctant to take any substantive action to provide permanent status to Liberian TPS beneficiaries. Instead, they have engaged in a yearly last minute reprieve routine that has left our people in a lingering state of hopelessness.

Living in this immigration limbo is heart-wrenching for these hardworking men and women. While each one-year extension of the TPS designation brings short-term relief, it also brews an unsettling degree of uncertainty for the future. The anxiety and stress of continuing to live in persistent fear of an inevitable disruption in their lives cannot be overemphasized. As is widely known, the majority of the people in this unpleasant situation are professionals, homeowners, business owners, and most importantly, parents to American- born children. They form the core of a breed of Liberians that are so positively contributing to both their homeland, Liberia and their adopted country, America. Something must be urgently done to remedy their immigration plight.

Like the United States government has often rushed to do for other nationalities in similar circumstances, Liberians too deserve a fair shake on this issue. According to federal government records, as released by the office of the venerable Rhode Island Senator Jack Reed, from the time Liberians were initially granted TPS in 1991 to 2002, Congress passed a law that allowed 4,996 Poles, 387 Ugandans, 565 Afghanis and 1,180 Ethiopians to adjust their status. The 102nd Congress also passed a law to change the status of over 50,000 Chinese nationals who had been granted DED after the Tiananmen Square massacre. Also, within about that same time period, Congress passed the NACARA legislation that put 150,000 Nicaraguans, 5,000 Cubans, 200,000 El Salvadorans and 50,000 Guatemalans on the path to seeking permanency in their status.

In 1999, during the Balkan crisis, the Clinton Administration oversaw the swift evacuation of tens of thousands of ethnic Albanians who appeared vulnerable to the imminent dangers posed by marauding Serb forces. These refugees were then promptly given the opportunity to become permanent residents here in the United States. As a believer in the inviolability of life, I was personally relieved and thankful to the U.S. authorities for that yeoman humanitarian effort.

My personal feelings aside, these precedents beg the question: *America, why is the Liberian case so markedly different?* U .S. authorities must wake up to the truth in the late Dr. Martin Luther King's assertion that "the arc of the universe is long but it bends toward justice." It is my hope that in the not-too-distant future, Liberians on TPS will be recipients of that same judicious commitment that was so generously given to the Albanians, the Chinese, Cubans, El Salvadorians, Nicaraguans, and other groups.

Akin to the larger illegal immigration saga, the TPS question inherently engenders a host of implications. If the legal status of the TPS beneficiaries is ever allowed to expire, the drawback will be instant and far-reaching. In addition to the individuals and families that will be directly ruined, the U.S. government as well as the Liberian nation will also be adversely impacted. There aren't any doubts that in this tangled web of a situation, what is going to hurt one part, will by all indications, eventually hurt the others.

Impact on Individuals and Families

Individuals and families caught up in this nightmarish immigration situation will be exposed to dire emotional, financial, and physical challenges if their legal status is ever jeopardized. They will be uprooted from a country in which they have lived continuously for close to two decades. They will be denied the benefits of social security and other retirement plans they have faithfully contributed to for so many years. They will be forced into defaulting on mortgages, personal loans, and other commitments they have in the United States.

Some will be forced to abandon their educational pursuits. Others will be forced to leave behind their American-born children because they wouldn't want to subject these children to the harsh realities of what life in Liberia truly is. Worst of all, they all will be sentenced to a life characterized by stinging unemployment, lack of adequate medical care, lack of higher educational opportunities, hunger, and homelessness. They also will be deprived of the ability they have here in America to literally support tens if not hundreds of extended family members back home through the frequent remittances that are a standard operating procedure for immigrants in the United States. The ripple effect this will create across Liberia will be immeasurable.

U.S.A.'s Burden

Outside of risking the irk of the world for the unfair treatment of Liberians (considering what was done for other nationalities in similar situations), the United States stands to create more long term problems for itself if it ever rescinds the TPS designation and eventually attempts to deport Liberians enjoying this protection. While some of the people will voluntarily go home to Liberia to face a life of hardship and uncertainty, others will definitely choose to stay in the United States and live the life of undocumented immigrants. Yes, they will make that hard decision to live in the "shadows."

When that becomes the reality, America would have put itself in the not so pleasant position of tussling with an array of "shadowy-existence" related problems. Instead of paying the payroll taxes they now pay, these people will work "under the table" for cash. When they witness a crime or sense the potential for one to be committed they will shy away from calling the police for fear of inadvertently alerting the authorities to their immigration status. They will most likely drive without valid driver's licenses as attempting to get one could expose their illegal status in the United States. This will mean they will ply the roads without insurance which in turn will endanger all other motorists and pedestrians. Also, because they will no longer be able to acquire health insurance legally they most likely will not readily seek medical care. As a consequence, treatable contagious diseases could morph into huge public health epidemics that could substantially tax U.S. resources.

Even for those Liberians that will decide to voluntarily pack up and go home, the United States will not escape the wrath of the problems their move will generate. As most of them with American-born children might decide to take their kids along to Liberia, we have got to pause and wonder what will happen when those children come of age and decide to return to America. They will be coming back with minimal language skills, sub-par education compared to their American-reared and trained peers, different social/ cultural orientations, and a feeling of injustice for having been shortchanged in the first place. These realities will be a recipe for creating societal misfits that the American social service and legal systems will have to grapple with for a long time.

GOL's Burden

At the recent celebration of the 160th independence anniversary of the Republic of Liberia in Washington, D.C., Ambassador Charles Minor is reported to have said "Liberia is in no position to absorb them [TPS beneficiaries], the unemployment rate is 85 percent and even basic necessities are lacking. We don't have the housing for them, there has been years of destruction of our schools. Teachers have left the country. So we have a very serious problem." I could not agree more with the ambassador. Sending thousands of Liberians back home at this point is tantamount to deliberately crippling the gradual resuscitation efforts being made in returning the country to a viable democracy.

The sheer accommodation demands on the young government will be overwhelming. Absorbing these returnees into the workforce will be practically impossible as both the public and private sectors are woefully unprepared for such influx. With hundreds of thousands of extended family members losing the source of their livelihood by virtue of the return of their U.S.A. based relatives, the economic burden on the government will be acerbic. Incapacitated to meet those challenges, the government will be exposed to dealing with social unrests and a rising crime rate as the population engages in desperate attempts for survival. If this happens, the country could regress to the instability, lawlessness, and bloodshed that marked the warring years. All the gains we have made, some with America's help, would have been for naught.

Conclusion

There is no denying the nexus that exists among the interests of the constituent players in the TPS debate. From the individual and family beneficiaries to the United States Government to the Liberian Government, each stakeholder has a lot to be concerned about. That is why it is essential for there to be a concerted effort on the part of all to resolve the situation.

So far, there are encouraging indications that this will be possible after all. Senator Jack Reed and Representative Patrick Kennedy of Rhode Island and Senator Amy Klobuchar and most members of the Minnesota Congressional delegation are on board working assiduously in this regard. The Liberian ambassador and executives of ULAA are also very seriously vested in these efforts. My thanks go to them all. However, I truly believe that a high-powered representation from the Liberian government, possibly our president herself, will best present the case I have outlined herein to the United States White house.

Meanwhile, let all of us Liberians keep doing what we have always done: working diligently, staying law-abiding, paying our taxes and hoping that

America will do the right thing-quitting the issuance of reprieves and instead putting in place the necessary mechanism for our people to gain permanent residency.

****

For many years, the threat of forced repatriation from the U.S.A. to Liberia has hung over a great many fellow Liberians living in America under the Temporary Protected Status/Deferred Enforced Departure status. In 2009, as the specter of the U.S. government ending the program drew near once again, I wrote this article as an impassioned plea to the authorities (both in Liberia and America) to work toward giving these Liberians a measure of permanency in their immigration status.

The Multiplier Effect: TRC Making Believers of Liberians One Person at a Time

'The conflict between a process that is procedurally neutral and nonpartisan by statutory definition, but in reality is one that releases torrents of rage at injustice is both the TRC's strength and its weakest point." --- Beth S. Lyons (1997).

Liberia's Truth and Reconciliation Commission (TRC), from its very inception, has been viewed differently by different individuals and interest groups. Many see it as a process that will finally reconcile the many dissensions in Liberian society and eventually heal the deep-seated wounds inflicted by our national nightmare. Yet, others see it as a superficial attempt by the government designed to let "criminals" off the hook of justice. Truth be told, I am one of those that initially abhorred the TRC as a mechanism for reconciliation and healing. I felt that for genuine peace and unity to prevail in Liberia, there was a need to enforce retributive justice for crimes committed during the civil war.

'The problem of justice,' therefore, underscored my earlier lack of faith in the TRC process. It is clear that Truth and Reconciliation Commissions around the world, including our very own in Liberia, by their mandates, cannot undertake the legal proceedings required to neither arrive at verdicts nor prescribe punishments for egregious perpetrators of human rights abuses. I agree that it is important to document the facts of the abuses, but not being clothed with the authority to institute any form of punitive justice, presented the TRC, at least in my view, as largely incapable of doing anything to deter a future repeat of the   atrocities it is investigating.

Setting out to ascertain the "truth", like Charles Lerche argues in his article Truth Commissions and National Reconciliation: Some Reflections on Theory and Practice published in the May 2000 edition of Peace and Conflict Studies, is an issue of inherent "complexity and multiplicity." Lerche reasons, and I concur, that "all sides [in a war situation] have their own versions of the truth, of what really happened." As these "competing versions of history and the politics of memory play themselves out," the central issues of demands for justice and hopes for lasting reconciliation become a faint blip in the larger pool of overwhelming, not to mention, contrasting, testimonies and evidences. I believe, also, that there is a strong link between justice and peace and that we can never substitute justice with just "truth."

Cllr. Jerome J. Verdier, Chairman of the TRC was recently in the Twin Cities to address some of these concerns. Speaking at a town hall meeting of a cross section of Liberians at the Community Center in Brooklyn Center, he set out to define the very essence of the TRC's work in Liberia. He argued that as much as his commission did not have the statutory authority to punish, it does have the option, at the end of its work, of making binding recommendations for the prosecution of especially grievous crimes. In this vein, he said, while his commission is not bent on meting out punishment, it's term of reference is not inimical to bringing human rights violators to justice. In fact, the Chairman reminded the audience, "human rights will only be achieved in Liberia through public acknowledgement of the violations that occurred, followed by a comprehensive reparations, justice and institutional reform program."

He pointed out, however, that his commission's intent is aligned more with creating a dependable record of what transpired, establishing an organized platform for the victims to tell their stories, and recommending, at the end of the process, legislative and structural changes to avoid a repetition of past abuses. He argued further, that the mere act of establishing a record of those that were responsible for the atrocities provides some measure of accountability. After all, he reasoned, dealing with the past is a critical part of the process of getting former adversaries to progress toward a peaceful shared future in Liberia. To achieve this end, the Chairman stressed, the Commission is grappling with many challenges that are impeding the pace of its work. He cited poor communication and transportation infrastructure, limitation of resources in view of the demands and short time frame of the commission mandate, and the unforgiving six months of rain that impose formidable constraints. Even more challenging, he said, was the difficulty of reaching out to the majority of Liberians both within the country and in the Diaspora.

Outside of the logistical dimension of this difficulty, he said, the problem of convincing people to believe in the mission of the commission as a viable way forward is especially urgent. For him and his fellow commissioners to succeed, he contended, it would require each and every Liberian to serve as an extension of their public relations efforts. He said, as they reach out to individuals and groups through such forums as town hall meetings, it was their hope and expectation that attendees will spread the word to others regarding the commission's goal of "preparing people's hearts for contrition, forgiveness and reconciliation."

Such efforts, he maintained, are bound to spur a multiplier effect-a sort of massive public awareness campaign that will make believers out of people and thereby ensure mass participation in the commission's statement taking efforts. And that, he emphasized, is the crucial thrust of the entire undertaking; the more people that are willing to talk, the more complete and comprehensive the commission's final report will be. Ending the presentation, the Chairman hoped that by the end of the process "the foundation for a new Liberia that is at peace with itself, reconciled with its past, united in its diversity and humane in its justice" will have been firmly planted.

The chairman, by his discourse, made me a champion of the cause of restoration — repairing the harm by transforming the relationship between victims and perpetrators as opposed to vengeance. As he continuously cautioned, returning Liberia to a "nobler destiny" requires much more than just punishing the evil doers. It is about reconditioning people's minds to believe in, going forward, "a stable, democratic and accountable society that cherishes the ideals of peace, justice and the rule of law." We must now all, in our own ways, contribute to the realization of this vision.

As we reckon with the legacy of our painful past as a country, all of us must participate to bring the process of transition to civilized norms to a fruitful conclusion. Yes, we might not all be thrilled with the "non-judicial" nature of the process, but, at least, it should warm our hearts to know that in the end, it will serve as a rehabilitative therapy of sorts that will cleanse our souls of genocidal tendencies. After all is said and done, no one in Liberia should be able to say "I do not know what really happened." That, to me, is the beginning of forgiveness which is a prerequisite to true healing and reconciliation.

****

When President Johnson-Sirleaf constituted the Truth and Reconciliation Commission (TRC), I was among the many critics of the idea. In 2008, I had the chance to listen to TRC Chairman Jerome Verdier espouse the importance of the commission. This article resulted from that listening session.

Death Be Not Proud: A Tribute to G. Baccus Matthews

I was never a member of Baccus' Progressive Alliance of Liberia (PAL) for I was but a child when it came to pass. I also never was a member of his United People's Party (UPP) for by the time it was launched, I had grown into a young man whose totality of political views were somewhat different from those espoused by that party's platform.

These truths notwithstanding, I have always been an admirer of Gabriel Baccus Matthews — the man, the political thinker, the fearless crusader for the peoples' rights and rice. Yes, as proved by his succumbing to the cold hands of death, G. Baccus was mortal and, as such, had his flaws. There is no denying that. But as I remember him today, I do so in the larger context of the giant he was among men; one willing to challenge head-on, a menacing True Whig Party oligarchy that would stop at nothing to squash political dissent. As silent as he has been rendered by death so also he will remain vocal by virtue of his legacy left on the Liberian political landscape. His immortalized slogan "*In the Cause of the People, the Struggle Continues*" will persist to be, in my estimation, the single most powerful driver of the political debate in our fledgling democracy.

Baccus realized early on that the cause of the people superseded any other consideration on all negotiating fronts. He preached that message all of the time. He lived that belief most of the time, sometimes at the peril of his very life. So, when I was jolted by the sad news of his passing, I figured a personal tribute was in order. To accomplish that in a simple, yet dignified manner, I settled on rendering an explication of John Donne's poem *"Death Be Not Proud"* to the memory of this Liberian political icon. So, here we go:

> *When it comes to G. Baccus, I will say death be not proud for you are a benign force. You are but an ordinary fact of life and you will never be revered Oh death, you might consider yourself powerful and mighty and some people may agree with that, the truth is, when it comes to Brother Matthews, you are really inconsequential. Do you really think you have vanquished G. Baccus and led him to a state of nothingness? I am sorry to let you know, death, that your so-called triumph is a figment of your imagination. What you have actually done, death, is elevate this icon and*

enable him to step into the realm of perpetual existence.

Death, you are a fickle, passing moment from which G. Baccus will emerge energized and happier. Be not proud for you are a mere slave of "fate, tyrants, and desperate men" – like those G. Baccus so fearlessly challenged during his lifetime. Death, you are feeble and powerless against a giant like Gabriel Baccus Matthews.

G. Baccus is dead, yet he is fully alive. He will continue to live on in the nation's psyche and in the conscience of all well-meaning Liberians forever. Fare you well and rest in perpetual peace, G. Baccus Matthews.

****

This eulogy was written on September 7, 2007, on the solemn occasion of the passing of Gabriel Baccus Matthews, an iconic figure in Liberian political lore.

About the Author

Momoh Sekou Dudu comes from the village of Gordorlahun in north-western Liberia. The civil war of 1989 – 2003 forced him and his family into exile first, in Sierra Leone and then in the French-speaking nation of Guinea-Conakry. Momoh stayed in Guinea for six long years. While there, he worked as a refugee community leader, helping to organize and coordinate UNHCR's periodic distributions of food rations. Later, Momoh joined the International Rescue Committee (IRC)-sponsored refugee school system where he served as a teacher, registrar, and eventually Vice Principal at the Gueckedou Refugee High School.

In the fall of 1997, Momoh won a competitive scholarship to travel to the United States to continue his college education. He graduated from Marymount Manhattan College, a small Liberal Arts school in New York City with a B.A degree (cum laude) in Business Management in 1999. Momoh went on to obtain a Master of Business Administration (M.B.A) Degree with emphasis in finance from the Peter J. Tobin School of Business at Saint John's University in Queens, New York. At present, he is in the end stages of study for a doctoral degree in Public Administration at Hamline University in St. Paul, Minnesota.

Over the last decade, Momoh has been a full-time as well as adjunct faculty at several Minneapolis metro area colleges and universities including Brown College, Minnesota School of Business at Globe University, and Cardinal Stritch University. He has also taught at Grand Canyon University and the University of Phoenix Online Campuses where he has facilitated classes in Economic Theory, Finance, and International Trade. He is currently Chair of the Business Programs at the Brooklyn Center and Blaine campuses of the Minnesota School of Business at Globe University.

He is the author of the memoir, Harrowing December: Recounting a Journey of Sorrows and Triumphs (2014); and When the Mind Soars: Poems from the Heart (2016). He is currently finishing work on his debut novel, Forgotten Legacy, which he hopes to release in mid-2017.

Momoh lives in the Minneapolis, Minnesota suburb of Otsego with his wife Mamasu and their two young children: Sekou and Makessa.

Also by the Author:

Harrowing December: Recounting a Journey of
Sorrows & Triumphs (2014)

When the Mind Soars: Poems from the Heart (2016)

Coming soon:

Forgotten Legacy (2017)

MOMOH SEKOU DUDU
Educator, Writer, and Public Speaker